Nibbāna As Living Experience

The Buddha and the Arahant

Two Studies from the Pāli Canon

Lily de Silva

Buddhist Publication Society
Kandy • Sri Lanka

Published in 1996

Buddhist Publication Society
P.O. Box 61
54, Sangharaja Mawatha
Kandy, Sri Lanka

ISBN 955-24-0128-3

"Nibbāna As Living Experience" originally appeared in the *Sri Lanka Journal of Buddhist Studies* (Vol. I, 1987).

"The Buddha and the Arahant" originally appeared in *Prītidāna Mañjarī*, Mudliyar W.S. Gunawardena Commemoration Volume, edited by M.H.F. Jayasuriya, Dehiwela, Sri Lanka.

Typeset at the BPS
Text set in Palatino

Printed in Sri Lanka by
Karunaratne & Sons Ltd.
647, Kularatne Mawatha
Colombo 10

THE WHEEL PUBLICATION NO. 407/408

Nibbāna As Living Experience

Nibbāna is the culmination of the Buddhist quest for perfection and happiness. In order to understand the meaning of this term it is useful to refer to the verse attributed to Kisā Gotami when she saw Prince Siddhattha returning to the palace from the park on the eve of his great renunciation. She declared:

> *Nibbutā nūna sā mātā, nibbuto nūna so pitā,*
> *Nibbutā nūna sā nārī, yassāyam īdiso patī.*[1]
>
> "Happy/contented/peaceful indeed is the mother (who has such a son), happy indeed is the father (who has such a son), happy indeed is the woman who has such a one as her husband."

Nibbuta (from *nir + vṛ*) is often treated as the past participle of the verb *nibbāyati*, and *nibbāna* is the nominal form of that verb. It means happiness, contentment, and peace. *Nibbāyati* also means to extinguish, to blow out as in the blowing out of a lamp.[2] Nibbāna is so called because it is the blowing out of the fires of greed, hatred, and delusion (*rāgaggi, dosaggi, mohaggi*).[3] When these fires are blown out peace is attained, and one becomes completely cooled—*sītibhūta*.[4] It is sometimes conjectured that Nibbāna is called cool because the Buddha preached in a warm country, where the cool was appreciated as comfortable. Had he taught in a cold climate, he might have described Nibbāna in terms of warmth. But it is certain that the term "cool" was chosen to convey a literal psychological reality.[5] Anger makes us hot and restless. We use expressions such as "boiling with anger," and they clearly express the intensity of the aggressive emotion. When such negative emotions are completely eradicated, never to arise again, the temperament has to be described as cool.

Nibbāna is a state to be attained here and now in this very life[6] and not a state to be attained only after death. In terms of *living experience* Nibbāna can be characterized by four special attributes: happiness, moral perfection, realization, and freedom. We shall take these up for discussion one by one.

Happiness

Nibbāna is described as the highest happiness, the supreme state of bliss.[7] Those who have attained Nibbāna live in utter bliss, free from hatred and mental illness amongst those who are hateful and mentally ill.[8] *Sukha* in Pāli denotes both happiness and pleasure. In English happiness denotes more a sense of mental ease while pleasure denotes physical well being. The Pāli word *sukha* extends to both these aspects and it is certain (as will be shown below) that mental and physical bliss is experienced by one who has attained Nibbāna.

The experience of non-sensuous physical bliss for limited periods is possible even before the attainment of Nibbāna through the practice of *jhāna* or meditative absorption. The Sāmaññaphala Sutta describes these physical experiences with the help of eloquent similes.[9] When bath powder is kneaded with water into a neat wet ball, the moisture touches every part of the ball but does not ooze out; similarly, the body of the adept in the first jhāna is drenched and suffused with joy and pleasure born of detachment from sense pleasures (*vivekajaṁ pītisukhaṁ*). The experience in the second jhāna is elucidated with a different simile. A deep pool filled to the brim with clear cool water is fed by underground springs, yet the waters do not overflow and no part of the pool remains untouched by the cool waters. Similarly joy and pleasure born of concentration (*samādhijaṁ pītisukhaṁ*) pervade the body of the meditator in the second jhāna. The simile for the third jhāna is a lotus born in water, grown in water, fully submerged in water, and drawing nourishment from water, with no part of the lotus remaining untouched by the cool water. Thus happiness/pleasure suffuses, drenches, and permeates the entire body of the adept in the third jhāna. These are the experiences of non-sensuous pleasure before the attainment of Nibbāna. On the attainment of Nibbāna more refined non-sensuous pleasure is permanently established. The Caṅkī Sutta specifically states that when a monk realizes the ultimate truth, he experiences that truth "with the body."[10]

Regarding the experience of the arahant, the Suttanipāta states that by the destruction of all feelings/sensations a monk lives desireless and at peace.[11] Once Sāriputta was asked what happiness there can be when there is no feeling/sensation.[12] He explained that the absence of feeling/sensation itself is happiness.[13] It is relevant to note here that the Buddha says that he does not speak of happiness only with reference to pleasant feelings/sensations. Wherever there is happiness or pleasure, that he recognizes as happiness or pleasure.[14]

Here we are reminded of the statement that all mental states converge on feelings.[15] What is meant by this statement seems to be that all mental states are translated into sensations in the body. It is possible to understand the import of this statement if we pay attention to a gross emotion, such as anger. When we are angry we experience a variety of bodily sensations: feeling hot, being restless, breaking out in a sweat, trepidation, etc. When we are sad, tears come into our eyes. These are brought about by changes in body chemistry through the discharge of various glandular secretions. If intense emotions bring about such gross sensations, we might conjecture that all thoughts cause subtle sensations in the body resulting from changes in body chemistry. We are hardly aware of these sensations which, however, become noticeable with the development of *vedanānupassanā*, contemplation of sensations. Thoughts are endless and continuous; therefore, if this interpretation that thoughts are translated into sensations is correct, sensations too should be endless and continuous. The Vedanāsaṁyutta states that just as diverse winds constantly blow in different directions, numerous sensations pass through the body.[16]

An arahant has full control over his thoughts;[17] therefore he must have full control over his feelings/sensations too. What is meant by the statement that "a monk lives desireless and at peace by the destruction of all feelings/sensations" seems to be that he has destroyed all psychogenic feelings/sensations. This leads us to another statement: that all feelings/sensations partake of the nature of suffering.[18] In order to understand the significance of this statement we must pay attention to our postures. If we have to remain seated for some time, say for an hour, we are not even aware of how many times we shift and adjust our limbs to more comfortable positions. This happens almost mechanically, as all the time we unconsciously seek to avoid discomfort. This is because monotony of sensations, even pleasant sensations, brings about discomfort and a change brings about a temporary sensation of comfort. If there were no sensations produced from within perhaps we would not need to change positions so often and we would have a running sense of ease even if we continue to remain in the same position for a long time.

Here it might be asked whether an arahant has lost the ability to feel pain, which is also an essential part of the touch sensation. It has to be pointed out that this is not so, for in that case an arahant would not even know if a part of his body is seriously injured or burnt. There is plenty of evidence to show that an arahant does feel sensations caused by physical changes. For instance, the Buddha felt acute pain when he was wounded by a stone splinter[19] and when he suffered from indigestion.[20] But he was able to withstand the painful sensations with mindfulness and clear comprehension without being fatigued by them. Again, an experience of Sāriputta throws light on the subject.[21] His experience refers to events which modern psychology designates as "non-ordinary reality of altered states of consciousness." A *yakkha*, a malevolent spirit, once gave Sāriputta a blow on the head. The blow, it is said, was so powerful that it was capable of splitting a mountain peak or making a seven and a half cubit high elephant go down on its knees. Moggallāna, who saw the incident with his divine eye, inquired from Sāriputta how he was feeling. He replied that he was all right, but there was slight pain in the head. This shows us that a blow which could have deprived an ordinary person of life had only minimal impact on an arahant.

Perhaps because the psychological factors which predispose a person to the experience of sensations are perfectly well under control in an arahant, he experiences only those sensations that are felt purely physically by an animate organism. It seems as if the body is under some sort of mentally regulated anesthesia which allows a narrow margin of sensation to protect the body from external danger. There are two kinds of pain, physical and mental,[22] and arahants are said to experience only physical pain,[23] without the anxious mental agony when experiencing physical pain.

It is also possible to look at this issue from another angle. Though the texts state that *vedanā* is destroyed in the arahant, they never say that the sense faculties are destroyed. When describing the super-conscious state of *saññā-vedayitanirodha*, the sense faculties are said to be refined—*vippasannāni indriyāni.*[24] So in the case of the arahant, too, the sense faculties must certainly be refined and not rendered deficient in any way. In that case it is possible to surmise that, though *vedanā* is extinct, body-sensitivity continues to be active and is thoroughly refined.

The Vedanāsaṁyutta differentiates between three types of joy and pleasure:[25]

(1) *Sāmisā pīti sāmisaṁ sukhaṁ*: joy and pleasure stimulated by sense objects, e.g. worldly sense pleasures.

(2) *Nirāmisā pīti nirāmisaṁ sukhaṁ*: Joy and pleasure free from stimulation by sense objects, e.g. jhānic experiences.

(3) *Nirāmisatarā pīti nirāmisataraṁ sukhaṁ*: more refined joy and pleasure free from stimulation by sense objects, e.g. Nibbāna.

An arahant experiences both physical and mental bliss (*so kāyasukham pi cetosukham pi paṭisaṁvedeti*) as all tensions (*darathā*), torments (*santāpā*), and fevers (*pariḷāhā*) have been completely eliminated for good.[26]

Bhaddiya was a monk who often exclaimed "What happiness, what happiness!" (*aho sukhaṁ aho sukhaṁ*). This expression of joy was misunderstood by his less developed fellow monks and they reported the matter to the Buddha, suspecting that Bhaddiya was often reminiscing about his lay comforts. On being questioned by the Buddha Bhaddiya explained that he was a prince in his lay life and that he had armed guards stationed in all strategic points within and without his palace, yet still he suffered from insomnia and insecurity, fearing that rivals might usurp his position and even deprive him of his life. But now, though living all alone in the open air, he is completely free from fear and anxiety. Therefore, to express his happiness, he frequently exclaimed: "What happiness, what happiness!"[27]

So great was the experience of joy on the attainment of release from all mental intoxicants (*āsavakkhaya*) that sometimes arahants have stayed in that same position continuously without moving for seven days enjoying the bliss of emancipation.[28] It is said that the whole body was permeated with this joy and bliss.

Thus there are various passages in the Pāli Canon which record the experience of bliss in the attainment of Nibbāna. But it appears that this bliss is not confined to or dependent on the five aggregates which constitute the individual. For the Dvayatānupassanā Sutta maintains that suffering (*dukkha*) ceases to arise with the cessation of the five aggregates.[29] Further, it is said in the Alagaddūpama Sutta that the perfected being (*tathāgata*) cannot be identified with any of the five personality factors even while he is still alive.[30]

Moral Perfection

Nibbāna is a state of moral perfection. For one who has attained Nibbāna, all unwholesome motivational roots such as greed, hatred, and delusion have been fully eradicated with no possibility of their ever becoming active again. Therefore Nibbāna is called the destruction of greed, hatred and delusion (*rāgakkhaya, dosakkhaya, mohakkhaya*). All inflowing moral depravities are destroyed, hence the epithet *āsavakkhaya* for Nibbāna. Craving has been uprooted for good, therefore *taṇhakkhaya* is another synonym. All types of conceit, the superiority and the inferiority complex plus the complex of equality (*seyyamāna, hīnamāna,* and *sadisamāna*), are eliminated. This necessarily has to be so as an arahant has no egoistic delusions such as I and mine. Just as much as an arahant has transcended egoism, he has transcended sexuality too. When Somā, a female arahant, was rebuked by Māra the Evil One, saying that womankind with very little intelligence cannot attain that state which is to be attained with great effort by seers and sages, Somā replied that womanhood is no impediment for the realization of truth to one who is endowed with intelligence and concentration.[31] Further, she adds that Māra must address these words to one who thinks "I am a man" or "I am a woman" and not to one like herself. This reply seems to imply that one loses even sexual identity on the attainment of arahantship.

There is evidence that an arahant has undergone such transformation in body chemistry that he has gone beyond the dichotomy of masculinity and femininity. All normal physiological sexual functions seem to be atrophied in an arahant as it is said that seminal emission is impossible for an arahant even in sleep.[32] We may also note the tradition maintaining that arahants never dream,[33] maybe because they have attained such perfect mental health that there is no necessity to release tension through dreams.

The sublime modes of conduct (*brahmavihāra*) such as lovingkindness, compassion, sympathetic joy, and equanimity (*mettā, karuṇā, muditā, upekkhā*) are fully developed without any limitations. An arahant is such a perfect being that it is simply impossible for him to commit an immoral act. He is incapable of wilfully destroying the life of a living creature. It is impossible for him to stoop so low as to steal something, to indulge in sex, to utter a deliberate lie, or to enjoy accumulated goods as in the household life.[34] One may wonder why household life is an impossibility for an arahant. The reason may be that the household is recognized as a fortress of greed where we deposit all *our* belonging; it is, in other words, the external repository of our ego. An arahant, who has fully transcended the ego, is incapable of partaking of such an institution.

Realization

Several expressions are used in the Pāli Canon to denote the cognitive aspect of the experience of Nibbāna. "The mass of darkness (of ignorance) has been torn asunder" (*tamokkhandhaṁ padālitaṁ*)[35] is a frequent expression. In his First Sermon the Buddha describes the realization of the Four Noble Truths as the arising of the eye, wisdom, insight, knowledge, and light.[36] "The three knowledges have been attained" (*tisso vijjā anuppattā*) is another expression.[37] The triple knowledge consists of retrocognition (*pubbenivāsānussatiñāṇa*), clairvoyance (*dibbacakkhu*), and the knowledge of the destruction of defilements (*āsavakkhayañāṇa*). With the first two knowledges one obtains personal verification of the doctrines of rebirth and kamma respectively. With the destruction of intoxicants one realizes the causal origination of all phenomena and egolessness.[38] Sometimes three other cognitive faculties (*abhiññā*) are mentioned as extra qualifications of arahants, namely, miraculous powers (*iddhividha*), the divine ear (*dibbasota*), and telepathy (*cetopariyañāṇa*).[39] With the attainment of Nibbāna one also realizes that birth is destroyed, the higher life has been successfully lived, one's duty has been done, and there is no more of this (mundane) existence.[40]

The Uddesavibhaṅga Sutta explains the nature of consciousness and the general cognitive attitude of an arahant:[41]

(1) The consciousness of an arahant is not scattered and diffused in the external world (*bahiddhā viññāṇaṁ avikkhittaṁ avisaṭaṁ*); this becomes possible because he does not indulge in the enjoyment of sense objects.

(2) His consciousness is not established within (*ajjhattaṁ asaṇṭhiṭaṁ*): this is possible because he does not become attached to the enjoyment of the jhānas.

(3) He remains unagitated without grasping (*anupādāya na paritassati*): this means that he does not identify himself with any of the five aggregates or personality factors.

The Mahāsaḷāyatanika Sutta explains more fully the cognitive experience of an arahant from the angle of sense experience.[42] The arahant realistically understands the nature of sense faculties, sense objects, sense consciousness, sense contact established by the convergence of these three factors, and the resulting sensations of pleasure, pain, and hedonic neutrality. He does not get attached to any of these factors. When he lives without deriving pleasure and without getting attached to perceived sense objects and without being deluded by the process of sense perception, recognizing the evil consequences of sense perception, the five aggregates of grasping or the personality factors do not get built up. They fall apart, as craving which leads to rebirth is totally eliminated. All physical and mental tensions (*darathā*), torments (*santāpā*), and fevers (*pariḷāhā*) are destroyed. The arahant experiences perfect physical and mental bliss.

We are not quite sure exactly what is meant by the realistic understanding of the nature of sense faculties, but we might suppose that an arahant intuitively understands, through the framework of his own personality, how the sense stimuli pass through sense receptors and nerve fibres and are interpreted at brain centres. Modern science explains to a certain extent the physiological processes involved in the activity of sense perception, but this understanding is confined at best to the intellectual level and is dependent on technological devices in medical laboratories. Such knowledge cannot bring about the attitudinal and emotional changes which are necessary for liberation. An arahant's understanding springs from a deeper experiential level with direct vision into the whole perceptual process as explained, for instance, in the Madhupiṇḍika Sutta.[43]

What is meant by the realistic understanding of sense objects? Most likely it is the realization of the impermanent, unsatisfactory, and non-substantial nature of all that is around us. This too is a direct profound experience of acute sensitivity, a direct personal vision into the dynamism of atomic and sub-atomic particles that go to form the material world around us as well as our bodies.

The Dhammapada records that when a monk sees in his contemplations the dynamic working of the physical and mental phenomena composing his own personality, great joy arises in him, and that can only be described as superhuman joy.[44] One has direct insight into the inner workings of one's body, the arising and passing away of body cells, sensations, perceptions, activities, and consciousness. Great is the joy and delight of this realization, and it is the realization of deathlessness.[45] This is what is called the "bliss of enlightenment" (*sambodhisukha*).

Freedom

All bonds which tie us down to suffering are torn asunder; thus Nibbāna is called *saṁyojanakkhaya*.[46] As the arahant has complete mastery over his thoughts (*cetovasippatta*),[47] no recurring unhealthy thoughts obsess him. Negative emotions restrict an individual's psychological freedom; therefore greed, hatred, and ignorance are described as *pamāṇakaraṇa*, i.e. they circumscribe an individual's freedom.[48] Greed, hatred, and ignorance are roots of unwholesome mental states which fetter the individual within *saṁsāra*.

There is an interesting simile which illustrates the nature of a fetter.[49] If there is a white bull and a black bull tied together by a rope, the question is asked, whether the white bull is a fetter to the black bull or the black bull is a fetter to the white bull. In fact neither is a fetter to the other; the fetter is the rope by which they are tied together. Similarly the desire we have for external objects is the fetter that binds us. The arahant has cut this off and attained freedom.

Unhealthy negative emotions are always self-oriented and self-centred. The Dhammapada says that the fool laments,

"He abused *me*, he beat *me*, he defeated *me*, he robbed *me*," and generates anger.[50] As he is firmly tied to the idea of the self or the ego, and he cannot wean himself away from the experience which inflicted a wound on his ego, he is like a dog tied to a post. This situation is quite in contrast to an experience the Buddha had once.[51] A brahmin came and abused him in very harsh language. The Buddha remained silent. When at last the brahmin stopped, the Buddha asked: "If you were to visit a friend and you took a gift to him, but the friend declined to accept the gift, what would you do?" The brahmin replied that he would take it back. The Buddha said: "You brought me a gift of much abuse, I do not accept; you can take it back." The Buddha also states that even if one is cut into pieces with a double-handled saw, one should train oneself not to generate anger towards the tormentor.[52] Moggallāna was an arahant who was mercilessly beaten by robbers but he was able to maintain his composure without a trace of anger. Such is the freedom one gains from negative emotions on the attainment of Nibbāna.

An arahant has fully developed the *brahmavihāras*, the sublime modes of conduct—universal love, compassion, sympathetic joy, and equanimity. These positive qualities are generated by transcending the self and are described as all-embracing and immeasurable (*appamāṇa*).[53] Thus they do not limit the scope of psychological freedom as do the mental states rooted in greed, hatred, and ignorance (*pamāṇakaraṇa*). The freedom won by an arahant is called *cetovimutti* and *paññāvimutti*, release of mind and release through wisdom. Knowledge also arises in the meditator that freedom has been gained (*vimuttasmiṁ vimuttam iti ñāṇaṁ hoti*). This is called the "bliss of emancipation" (*vimuttisukha*), the highest bliss that any human being could enjoy.

Creativity

Creativity is another aspect under which the achievement of an arahant can be fruitfully discussed. The virtues of the arahant can be succinctly summarized as *karuṇā* and *paññā*, compassion and wisdom. These are the two qualities through which the creativity of the arahant finds expression. When arahants look at humanity they are moved by great compassion as they fully realize the gravity of the precarious condition of the worldlings. Therefore, they willingly plunge into a life of selfless activity, preaching to the people, trying to show them the path leading out of misery to eternal peace. It is especially noteworthy that the Buddha's role as teacher was so demanding that he barely slept two hours a day. The body of discourses he gave during the course of his long ministry of forty-five years is as profound as it is extensive. It stands preeminent in world literary history for originality of ideas, profundity of thought, and clarity of expression. These observations hold good for the discourses delivered by the arahants as well. The entire Pāli Canon can be considered as testimony to the creative genius of the liberated beings. It is but natural that creativity finds spontaneous expression when a person attains liberation, as all negative emotions which hinder creativity and distort spontaneity are totally eliminated in the arahant.

Some arahants are endowed with the special accomplishment of the fourfold analytical knowledge (*paṭisambhidā-ñāṇa*), which qualifies them even more thoroughly for creative work.[54] These are spelt out as analytical knowledge of the meaning or goal, profound truth, language or the medium of communication, and originality of expression (*attha, dhamma, nirutti, paṭibhāna*). These four special qualifications make arahants experts in communicating to their audience the exact meanings and goals of the profound truths they have discovered, through the medium of refined language, using their own original modes of expression such as eloquent similes, metaphors, etc. Several arahants, both male and female, are recorded as eloquent speakers and erudite exponents of the Dhamma.[55] Special mention must be made of the Theragāthā and Therīgāthā, which comprise poems of exquisite beauty. They are utterances of monks and nuns embodying their varied experiences. Literary critics rank them among the best lyrics in Indian literature.[56] They remain unrivalled in the literary history of the world as creative writing issuing forth from the undefiled purity of the human heart and the nobility of human wisdom. They are ever-fresh fountains of inspiration to the truth-seeker and lasting monuments to the creatve genius of the liberated beings.

Physiology and Spirituality

Having considered this traditional material from the Pāli Canon let us now turn to modern studies on psycho-physiology and meditation to see whether we can draw some inferences from them on the experience of Nibbāna.

Studies done by investigators such as Walter B. Canon show beyond doubt that there is a definite correlation between physiology and strong emotions.[57] "When a sensory trunk is strongly excited the adrenal glands are reflexly stimulated and they pour into the blood stream an increased amount of adrenalin."[58] This gives rise to the overt manifestation of bodily changes such as dilation of the pupils, sweating, rapid respiration, etc.[59] There are other physiological changes such as those in heart beat, blood pressure, blood volume, electrodermal responses, etc.[60] But they are not quite useful for us as they cannot be related to material found in the Pāli Canon. The logical inference is that if strong negative emotions can give rise to certain physiological changes in the body, changes which may be described as unhealthy, the cultivation of positive emotions too should give rise to physiological changes which are quite different from those stimulated by negative emotions.

As opposed to the dilation of the pupils and a consequent look of ferocity in the instance of a strong emotion such as anger, we find in the Pāli texts mention made of the monks' eyes as being very pleasant. The monks, it is said, look at one another with amiable eyes and they mix with one another as milk and water blend.[61] This feature was conspicuous enough to draw the attention of the intelligent public; for example, King Pasenadi Kosala cited the pleasing expression in the eyes of the monks as one of the special characteristics which convinced him that they possess purity of heart and spiritual maturity.

The complexion or facial expression of the monks is also mentioned as an impressive feature indicating the height of spirituality attained. The bright clear complexion or serene facial expression[62] attracted the attention of many observers and inspired their confidence in the Dhamma. For instance, Sāriputta was impressed by the bright countenance and the serene appearance of the monk Assaji, and that was the starting point of his conversion.[63] King Asoka's conversion to Buddhism was prompted by the outward appearance of the novice Nigrodha.[64] The spotlessly pure bright complexion of the Buddha was counted as one of the thirty-two marks of a great man and these marks are considered the outward manifestations of profound spiritual maturity.[65]

As sweating is one of the physiological manifestations of emotional excitement, there is an interesting incident from the life of the Buddha relevant for our present study. Once Saccaka, a redoubtable debater, came for a debate with the Buddha. He boasted that he would harass the Buddha in debate as a strong man would shake a goat to and fro while holding it by its long beard. Arrogantly he bragged that he could see no man who would not break out in a sweat when challenged by him in debate. But when the debate with the Buddha was actually held before a large audience it was Saccaka who sweated profusely in defeat. The Buddha bared his chest and showed that he did not sweat at all.[66] This episode may be taken as evidence that an arahant does not perspire due to emotional excitement.

Rapid respiration is another physiological accompaniment of negative emotions. Changes in breathing rhythm or amplitude are considered excellent indicators of deception.[67] It is a commonplace experience that respiration remains calm and placid when we are quiet and resting. It becomes even calmer in meditation. The Pāli Canon maintains that respiration ceases altogether during the fourth jhāna, which is a subtle, highly refined state of superconsciousness.[68] It is possible that metabolism comes to a standstill or a minimum level during this state. Though arahants do not always abide in this jhāna, they must constantly maintain a calm regular rhythm in their respiration, for they never become emotionally disturbed or excited. Their calm is so profound that it is said that they also maintain an inner silence even when they speak, as the sub-vocal chatter which is characteristic of others has been quelled altogether in their case.[69]

Modern scientific studies on the physiology of meditation shed light on some other aspects relevant to the present study. It has been found that the concentration of blood-lactate level declines precipitously in meditation.[70] Its concentration normally falls in a subject at rest but the rate of decline during meditation has proved to be more than three times faster than the normal rate.[71] This offers a good contrast to the rise of blood-lactate levels when patients with anxiety neurosis are placed under stress.[72] It is also reported from experiments that the infusion of lactate brings about attacks of anxiety in such patients. Furthermore, it is significant that patients with hypertension (essential and renal) show higher blood-lactate levels in a resting state than patients without hypertension, whereas in contrast, the low lactate level in meditators is associated with low blood pressure.[73] Thus it is clear that the fall in the blood-lactate level has a beneficial psychophysiological effect. All this medical evidence goes to show that a calm healthy mind finds expression in a positively transformed body chemistry. Therefore it is reasonable to maintain that one who has reached the culmination of meditative practice and realized Nibbāna is healthy in both mind and body.

The body has certain electrical properties that are clearly associated with psychological processes such as attention and emotion.[74] One of these is shown in the rapid rise in the electrical resistance of the skin accompanying meditation. Wallace and Benson report that fifteen subjects tested showed a rise of about 140,000 ohms in 20 minutes.[75] In sleep, skin resistance normally rises, but not so much or at such a rate.[76] The same test is used in lie detection, and most laboratory studies have found that the skin resistance response is the best indicator of deception.[77] This evidence shows beyond doubt that involuntary physiological changes accompany emotional states both positive and negative. Again it is said that the brain is constantly emitting small electrical potentials measured in cycles per second called Hertz (Hz). These waves of varying frequencies and shapes are labelled with Greek letters such as delta waves (less than 4 Hz), theta waves (4–7 Hz), alpha waves (8–13 Hz), and beta waves (greater than 14 Hz).[78] Electro-encephalographic recordings of subjects in meditation have disclosed a marked intensification of alpha waves. Wallace and Benson report that they recorded the waves from seven main areas of the brain on magnetic tape and analysed the patterns with a computer. They say that typically there was an increase in intensity of slow alpha waves at eight or nine cycles per second in the frontal and central regions of the brain during meditation. In several subjects this change was also accompanied by prominent theta waves in the frontal areas.[79] On the other hand, emotional disturbance such as anger is always accompanied by alpha blocking whereas sleep, "the antithesis of emotion," is characterized by slow high-amplitude activity. Light and sound stimuli also block the alpha rhythm. It is reduced or suppressed during periods of apprehension. Alpha waves are absent in records of patients in an anxiety state.[80] On the strength of these findings it is possible to conjecture that the harmony of the mind determines to a very large extent the health of the body.

When related to the experience of Nibbāna it seems reasonable to conjecture that an arahant has put an end to all psychosomatic diseases. His body would be susceptible only to physical ailments and injury caused by external agents. There are reports in the Pāli Canon of arahants falling ill and experiencing acute pain.[81] It is also noteworthy that they are said to have recovered by meditating on the Dhamma. On the strength of the evidence furnished so far one is inclined to regard their illnesses as being caused by physiological factors. There is also an incident of a monk who is not an arahant dying of snakebite. The Buddha says that if the monk had practised *mettā* fully he would not have met with such an unfortunate death.[82] It may be that the snake would not have bitten him in the first place had *mettā* been fully cultivated. On the other hand, there is another commentarial episode where a non-arahant monk was bitten by a poisonous snake while he was listening to the Dhamma.[83] The poison started spreading in the body and the pain became acute. The monk then reflected on the immaculate purity of his virtues from the time he received higher ordination. It is said that, as a result of this reflection, great joy arose in his mind suffusing his entire body. The joy acted as an anti-venom and he was cured.

Meditation is described in psychophysiological terminology as a "wakeful hypometabolic" state characterized by: "reductions in oxygen consumption, carbon dioxide elimination, and the rate and volume of respiration; a slight increase in the acidity of arterial blood; a marked decrease in the blood-lactate level; a slowing of the heart beat; a considerable increase in skin resistance; and an electro-encephalogram pattern of intensification of slow alpha waves with occasional theta-wave activity."[84] It may be surmised that the metabolism during normal waking hours is probably maintained at the lowest possible healthy level in the case of the arahant, as his body is not subject to undue wear and tear brought about by emotional excitement. The positive refined sublime emotions or the divine modes of conduct (*brahmavihāra*) such as *mettā, karuṇā, muditā,* and *upekkhā,* not to speak of the higher cognitive states, must necessarily find expression in body chemistry to produce a healthy constitution and a calm, unruffled, serene personality filled with peace, contentment, and the joy of enlightenment (*sambodhisukha*).

We are reminded here of a statement the Buddha once made. He said that even if there is a portion as small as a pinch of dust that defies change in the psychophysical personality of the human being, leading the higher life (*brahmacariya*) would be useless.[85] What is meant is that there is no such permanent part and the higher life can successfully bring about a total transformation of the individual in both mind and body. Modern scientific studies on the physiology of meditation prove that basic biochemical and bioelectrical changes do take place in the body as a result of mental culture. It is therefore possible to surmise that mental culture culminates in a total psychophysical transformation.

Studies done on the bio-feedback technique suggest that a radical transformation of the nervous system must take place with the development of higher mental potentialities. It is common knowledge that the autonomous nervous system is divided into two parts, the sympathetic nervous system and the parasympathetic nervous system. Johann Stoyva, in an article on bio-feedback techniques, states that probably in deep relaxation there is a shift in the autonomous nervous system towards parasympathetic dominance. Parasympathetic functioning is associated with subtler emotions—wonder, religious and aesthetic experiences, contemplation—emotions characterized by a broader range of awareness.[86] On the other hand, sympathetc predominance is linked to emotions in which the range of awareness is restricted—anger and fear, for example. On the strength of this evidence it may be conjectured that parasympathetic functioning develops to greater efficiency with spiritual advancement.

Very little is known about the functions of the pineal gland, which René Descartes regarded as the chosen residence of the human soul. It is described as the built-in biological clock of the human being on which depends the regularity of sleeping and waking.[87] This gland synthesizes a hormone called *melatonin* which affects behaviour, sleep, brain activity, and sexual activity such as puberty, ovulation, and sexual maturation.[88]

While melatonin stimulates brain activity, it inhibits sexual activity. Again it has been recognized that light/dark, olfaction, cold, stress, and other neural inputs affect the pineal function.[89] Exposure to light reduces the synthesis of melatonin and depresses pineal weight.[90] On the other hand, light accelerates sexual maturation and activity.[91]

In the context of Buddhist thought the function of the pineal gland seems to be the biological basis of sense control. Buddhism maintains that unrestrained sense stimulation disturbs mental activity. If the sense doors are well guarded, i.e. if visual, auditory, olfactory, gustatory, and tactile imputs are controlled, a corresponding degree of happiness (*avyāseka-sukha*) and concentrated mental activity become possible.[92] *Cittass'ekaggatā*, the ability to fix the mind on one point, is greatly determined by the control of the sense faculties. In terms of physiology it seems that such sense control helps the synthesis of melatonin in the pineal gland which stimulates brain activity and retards sexual activity. Thus in terms of pineal function, brain activity and sexual activity seem to be antithetical. Buddhism, too, emphasizes that sexual desire prevents clear thinking, distorts vision, clouds issues, inhibits wisdom, and destroys peace of mind.[93]

The entire scheme of spiritual development comprising the Noble Eightfold Path is an efficient methodical plan of action designed to bring a gradual psychophysical transformation culminating in the attainment of Nibbāna. Cultivation of moral habits (*sīla*) is the frame for wholesome behaviour by means of which healthy body chemistry gets gradually established. Neural circuits related to harmonious physical and vocal activity are strengthened and those related to violence become proportionately weak. The second phase in the development of the Noble Eightfold Path comprises meditation. A steady rapid psychophysical development takes place during this phase. It is our conjecture that the adrenalin secretion which accompanied negative emotions of rage and fear is reduced to a healthy, workable level. Perhaps adrenalin is secreted in small quantities into the blood stream to maintain an unflagging enthusiasm to continue in the difficult practice of meditation with undaunted courage and perseverance. Or it may be, as the endocrine glands stimulate or inhibit one another, a balanced combination of these glandular secretions affects the cognitive and emotional behaviour of the meditator. When sublime modes of conduct such as *mettā, karuṇā, muditā,* and *upekkhā* are practised over and over again they must become ingrained in the nervous system, perhaps increasing parasympathetic dominance. With the practice of *vipassanā* or insight-meditation, the pineal gland seems to develop its full bodily potential for unlocking all possible spiritual knowledges in the meditator's mind and when the process is complete Nibbāna is attained.

This interpretation finds further support in the Buddhist conception of the reciprocal relationship between *viññāṇa* and *nāmarūpa*. This relationship is illustrated in the Canon with the simile of two bundles of reeds placed together supporting each other. A change of position in one is bound to make a corresponding change in the other. Thus psychological development affects physiological function, apparently through the activity of the nervous system and the endocrine glands. Healthy physiological changes reinforce healthy psychological activity. Thus the process of mutual psychophysical interaction works for the happiness or misery of the individual depending on the moral quality of the actions performed through body, speech, and mind. As the mind is involved in all activity it is the mind that is responsible for the quality of body chemistry and neural function.

When the mind ultimately attains to a state of absolute purity beyond corruptibility, body chemistry and neural function undergo a radical transformation which will not be reversed again. It can be conjectured that when the pineal gland and its auxiliaries develop to the fullest possible capacity, the hitherto inactive brain regions unlock their secrets and reveal them when attention is directed accordingly. Thus memory becomes so efficient as to revive prenatal knowledge running into numerous previous existences. Similarly, the divine eye, or clairvoyance, is clarified, disclosing the kammic antecedents of human experience. When one gains direct vision and knowledge of the bodily and mental processes involved in the human personality one attains supreme enlightenment.

The Avyākatas

The state of Nibbāna after the death of the arahant is nowhere discussed in the Pāli Canon. The four alternatives put forward regarding this state, namely: Does the Perfect One exist after death, does he not, does he and does he not, does he neither exist nor not exist after death, are all left aside unanswered. These questions are put aside because they are not useful to human happiness and understanding, not concerned with the Dhamma, not helpful for the higher life, not conducive to disenchantment and detachment, not conducive to cessation of misery, to tranquillity of the mind, to higher knowledge, to insight, and to peace (Nibbāna).[94]

The Aggivacchagotta Sutta cites a simile in this connection which illustrates that the questions themselves are meaningless.[95] If there is a fire burning and if the fire goes out without fuel, can one ask the question: "In which direction did the fire go, east, south, west, or north?" The question itself is inappropriate as it assumes that fire can have existence independent of fuel. The nun Khemā points out that the state of the Tathāgata after death is immeasurable. Just as it is impossible to calculate the drops of water in the ocean and the grains of sand in the earth, so is it impossible to conceptualize the state of Nibbāna after the demise of the arahant.[96] The Anurādha Sutta states that the five aggregates of grasping, or the personality factors, are impermanent, unsatisfactory, and non-self. Therefore the noble disciple is detached from them. He wins freedom, and after death becomes completely untraceable.[97] The Alagaddūpama Sutta maintains that the Tathāgata cannot be identified with the personality factors even during his lifetime, so how can he be identified after death?[98]

A plausible explanation is necessary for the traditional silence regarding the state of the arahant after death. Existence in the world implies time and space. One exists within a particular period in a particular space or locality. If one passes beyond time and beyond space, it is not possible to speak of existence with reference to such a one. To speak of both time and space one needs a point of reference, e.g. A is 50 years old. This means 50 years have passed since the event of A's birth. If A is not born, it is impossible to speak of "time" or existence with reference to him. Similarly with space. Without points of reference it is not possible to grasp space. There is a definite distance between any two specific points. Nor can one speak of direction without a point of reference. When the notion of "I," which is the point of personal reference, is eradicated, one goes beyond time, beyond space, and beyond causality. Therefore it is not possible to speak of the liberated being as existing or not existing.

Here we are reminded of a statement made by Fritjof Capra in his *Tao of Physics* relevant to our present context. He states: "Physicists can 'experience' the four dimensional space-time world through the abstract mathematical formalism of their theories, but their visual imagination, like everybody else's, is limited to the three-dimensional world of the senses. Our language and thought patterns have evolved in this three-dimensional world and therefore we find it extremely hard to deal with the four-dimensional reality of relativistic physics."[99] Thus, when the four-dimensional reality too eludes the perceptual experience of the average man, how can Nibbāna, which transcends all these four dimensions, come within mere verbal experience? Therefore it is impossible to speak of the arahant's state in terms of existence or non-existence.

At this point an observation can be made from another point of view. Buddhism describes the characteristics of all things in three statements: *Sabbe saṅkhārā aniccā, sabbe saṅkhārā dukkhā, sabbe dhammā anattā* , meaning all conditioned things are impermanent, all conditioned things are unsatisfactory, all phenomena are non-self.[100] Here the change of terminology in the last statement seems important. The Saṁyutta Commentary explains the last statement as: *Sabbe dhammā anattā ti sabbe catubhūmakā dhammā.*[101] The *Visuddhimagga* explains the four *bhūmis* or planes as *kāmāvacara, rūpāvacara, arūpāvacara,* and *lokuttara,* meaning the sensual sphere, the fine-material sphere, the immaterial sphere, and the supramundane.[102] Therefore *dhammā* in our statement can be interpreted as including the supramundane state of Nibbāna as well. Commenting on this statement Ven. Nārada Thera observes: "*Dhammā* can be applied to both conditioned and unconditioned things and states. It embraces both conditioned and unconditioned things including Nibbāna. In order to show that even Nibbāna is free from a permanent soul the Buddha used the term *dhammā* in the third verse. Nibbāna is a positive supramundane state and is without a soul."[103] It is significant that *dhammā* was not used in the first two statements. The purpose seems to be to exclude Nibbāna which is permanent and blissful. Therefore we can surmise a condition that is permanent and blissful, but it is not a self. That state is Nibbāna. It has to be a dimension completely different from all that is worldly. The permanence that is conjectured here has no reference to time and space, and the bliss that is spoken of has no reference to feelings, *vedanā*.

Further, there is a great difference between the death of an ordinary worldling and that of an arahant. To indicate this, a different terminology is used: *maraṇa/miyyati* is used for the death of a worldling, while *parinibbāna/parinibbāyati* is used in the case of an arahant. In fact the Dhammapada specifically states that the vigilant ones, meaning arahants, never die (in the ordinary sense of the word).[104]

Let us first see what happens when a worldling dies. It is an accepted fact that everybody fears death.[105] We also fear the unknown; therefore death is doubly fearful because we know least about it. It seems reasonable to assume that at the root of all fear there lurks the fear of death. In other words we fear everything which directly or indirectly threatens our life. So long as our bodies are strong enough, we can either fight or run away from the source of fear, with the intention of preserving life. But when ultimately we are on the deathbed face to face with death and our body is no longer strong enough to flee from death, it is highly unlikely that we will mentally accept death with resignation. We will struggle hard, long for and crave for life (*taṇhā*), and reach out and grasp (*upādāna*) a viable base somewhere as the dying body can no longer sustain life. Once such a viable base, for instance a fertilized ovum in a mother's womb, has been grasped, the process of becoming or growth (*bhava*) starts there, which in due course gives rise to birth (*jāti*). This is what is referred to in the twelve-linked *paṭiccasamuppāda* as "craving conditions grasping, grasping conditions becoming, becoming conditions birth."[106] Thus a worldling dies and is reborn.

Now let us consider the last moments of an arahant. As an arahant has no fear whatsoever from any source (*akutobhaya*), he would not be agitated (*na paritassati*) as he has no craving for life.[107] He will watch the process of death with perfect equanimity and crystal-clear mindfulness.[108] Further, the Mahāparinibbāna Sutta, which explains the final moments of the Buddha, states that the Buddha passed away immediately after rising from the fourth jhāna.[109] The fourth jhāna is characterized by purity of equanimity and mindfulness.[110] It is not known whether all arahants attain *parinibbāna* after the fourth jhāna, but certainly they cannot have a deluded death.[111] As they do not grasp another birth the state they attain after final passing away has to be described as unborn (*ajāta*). Similarly it is uncaused (*asaṅkhata*).[112] As it is no ordinary death it is called the deathless state.[113] It is beyond elemental existence, beyond *brahmalokas*, neither in this world nor the next, beyond the radiance of the sun and moon.[114] It is beyond what we know of in the three worlds of *kāma*, *rūpa*, and *arūpa*. Therefore, as it is beyond the ken of ordinary human understanding, any attempt to define the state is bound to end in failure. The course of liberated ones cannot be traced like that of birds in the air.[115]

Notes

1. J I 60.
2. *Nibbanti dhīrā yathāyaṁ padīpo*: Sn 235.
3. S IV 19.
4. Sn 542, 642.
5. A I 138, III 435.
6. D I 156, 167.
7. *Nibbānaṁ paramaṁ sukhaṁ*: Dh 203.
8. *Susukhaṁ vata jīvāma verinesu averino/āturesu anāturā*: Dh 197-99.
9. D I 74.
10. *Kāyena c'eva paramasaccaṁ sacchikaroti*: M II 173.
11. *Vedanānaṁ khayā bhikkhu nicchāto parinibbuto*: Sn 739.
12. *Kim pan'ettha n'atthi vedayitaṁ ti*: A IV 415.
13. *Etad eva khv'ettha sukhaṁ yad ettha n'atthi vedayitaṁ.*
14. S IV 228.

15. *Vedanāsamosaraṇā sabbe dhammā*: A IV 339, V 107; *saṅkappavitakkā vedanāsamosaraṇā*: A IV 385.
16. S IV 218.
17. *Cetovasippatta*: A II 6, 36.
18. *Yaṁ kiñci vedayitaṁ taṁ dukkhasmin ti*: S IV 216.
19. Vin II 193.
20. D II 127.
21. Ud 40.
22. *Kāyikañ ca cetasikā ca*: S IV 231.
23. *Arahā ekaṁ vedanaṁ vediyati kāyikaṁ na cetasikan ti*: Miln 253.
24. M I 296.
25. S IV 235.
26. M III 288–89.
27. ThagA III 52.
28. *Pītisukhena ca kāyaṁ pharitvā vihariṁ tadā*
    Sattamiyā pāde pasāresiṁ tamokkhandhaṁ padāliya: Thig 274.
29. Sn pp.142–48.
30. M I 140.
31. S I 129.
32. *Aṭṭhānam etaṁ anavakāso yaṁ arahato asuci mucceyyā ti*: Vin I 295.
33. *Compendium of Philosophy* (London: PTS, 1956), p.50.
34. M I 523.
35. Thag 128.
36. *Cakkhuṁ udapādi ñāṇaṁ udapādi paññā udapādi vijjā udapādi āloko udapādi*: S V 424.
37. M II 105.
38. M I 55.
39. M II 18–22.
40. *Nāparaṁ itthattāyā ti pajānāti*: M I 67.
41. M III 223.

42. M III 287.
43. M I 111.
44. Dh 373.
45. Dh 374.
46. S II 186.
47. A II 6, 36.
48. M I 298.
49. S IV 162.
50. Dh 4.
51. S I 162.
52. M I 129.
53. D I 251.
54. A II 160.
55. A I 23, 25.
56. M. Winternitz, *Indian Literature*, Vol. II, p.100.
57. *Bodily Changes in Pain, Hunger, Fear and Rage* (Maryland: McGrath, 1970), pp.12–24.
58. Ibid., p.59.
59. Ibid., p.57.
60. William W. Grings and Michael E. Dawson, *Emotions and Bodily Responses* (New York: Academic Press, 1978), pp.12–24.
61. *Khīrodakībhūte aññamaññaṁ piyacakkhūhi sampassante viharante*: M II 121.
62. *Parisuddho chavivaṇṇo pariyodāto* : Vin I 8.
63. Vin I 41.
64. VinA I 45.
65. Lakkhaṇa Sutta, D I 143.
66. M I 233.
67. Grings and Dawson, pp.157–58.
68. S IV 217.

69. Sn 731, M I 301.
70. "The Physiology of Meditation" by Robert Keith Wallace and Herbert Benson, in *The Nature of Human Consciousness*, ed. Robert E. Ornstein (San Francisco: H.W. Freeman, 1973), p.262.
71. Ibid., p.262.
72. Ibid., p.264.
73. Ibid., p.265.
74. Grings and Dawson, p.16
75. *The Nature of Human Consciousness*, p.264.
76. Ibid., p.264.
77. Grings and Dawson, pp.156ff.
78. Ibid., p.19.
79. *The Nature of Human Consciousness*, pp.257, 265, 270.
80. S.P. Grossman, *Textbook of Physiological Psychology* (New York, 1967), pp.516–17.
81. S V 79–81; A V 108.
82. A II 72; Vin II 109.
83. MA I 78.
84. *The Nature of Human Consciousness*, p.266.
85. S III 147.
86. *The Physiology of Thinking: Studies in Covert Processes*, ed. E.J. McGuigan and R.A. Schoonover (N.Y.: Academic Press, 1973).
87. Nigel Calder, *The Mind of Man* (New York, 1970), p.36
88. *The Pineal Gland*, ed. G.E.W. Wolstenholme and Julie Knight (Ciba Foundation Symposium, London, 1971), pp.215, 368–372, 343, 268, 271–272.
89. Ibid., pp.384, 385.
90. Ibid., pp.381, 380.
91. Ibid., p.300.
92. D I 70.
93. A I 216; M I 115.
94. See e.g. D I 191.

95. M I 487.
96. S IV 374.
97. S IV 380.
98. M I 140.
99. p.150
100. Dh 277–79; S III 133.
101. SA II 318.
102. Vsm 454. A note of caution has to be added to this interpretation, as DhA III 407 explains: *tattha sabbe dhammā ti pañcakkhandhā va adhippetā ti*, "what is meant by all dhammas is precisely the five aggregates."
103. *The Dhammapada*, a translation by Ven. Nārada Thera, p.225, on v.279.
104. *Appamattā na mīyanti:* Dh 21.
105. *Sabbe bhāyanti maccuno* : Dh 129; also Vsm I 239.
106. *Taṇhāpaccayā upādānaṁ upādānapaccayā bhavo bhavapaccayā jāti.*
107. *Na kiñci loke upādiyati, anupādiyaṁ na paritassati, aparitassaṁ paccattaṁ yeva parinibbāyati*: D II 68; *anupādāya aparitassato āyatiṁ jātijarāmaraṇadukkhasamudayasambhavo na hoti*: M III 223.
108. *Upekhavā anupādāya ca na paritassati*: M III 228.
109. *Catutthajjhānā vuṭṭhahitvā samanantarā Bhagavā parinibbāyi*: D II 156.
110. *Upekkhāsatipārisuddhi*: D I 75.
111. *Sammohamaraṇa*: Vsm 314.
112. Ud 80.
113. *Amatapada*: Dh 21.
114. Ud 80.
115. *Ākāse va sakuntānaṁ gati tesaṁ durannayā*: Dh 92.

The Buddha and the Arahant

In the Gopakamoggallāna Sutta a brahmin asks the Venerable Ānanda whether there is a single monk who is completely endowed with all the qualities with which the Buddha is endowed. Ānanda replies that there is not a single monk who is so endowed.[1] In this paper an attempt is made to compare the attainments of the Buddha with those of the arahant, with a view to ascertain wherein the two differ.

Both the Buddha and the arahants are recognized as equal as far as the attainment of the final goal of Nibbāna is concerned. The principal difference is that the Buddha is the pioneer, the discoverer of the undiscovered path, while the arahants are followers who tread the path mapped out by the pioneering Buddha. The Cūḷagopālaka Sutta uses a slightly different allegory: it compares the Buddha to a clever cowherd who gets his herd to cross a deep river from a safe ford.[2] Later Buddhist texts elucidate the pioneership of the Buddha with lucid descriptions of how he spent incalculable periods of time practising and perfecting the virtues called *pāramitā,* which gave him the intellectual and emotional maturity to discover the long forgotten path to Nibbāna.[3] But it is specifically stated that the Buddha did not preach all that he understood during the process of preparation. What he preached is compared to a handful of leaves, whereas what he understood but refrained from teaching is like the leaves in the forest.[4] The Buddha also maintains that he preached the Dhamma in its entirety without any reservations.[5] What is meant by these superficially contradictory statements seems to be that the Buddha taught everything useful and relevant for emancipation, but kept strictly aside everything that was useless and irrelevant for that purpose. This position is reiterated in the Canon in a number of suttas. The Buddha clearly defined the scope of his teaching and strictly confined himself to the problem of suffering and its elimination.[6]

The Buddha's standpoint can be illustrated with the help of a simile. He was like a lonely man who was lost in the fearful wilderness of *saṁsāra* and earnestly sought a way out. As he had to spend a long time in this vast terrible forest he had to learn a great deal about the forest itself. To survive he had to learn about edible and poisonous plants and fruits; he had to learn the habits and habitats of wild animals; he had to climb trees in order to discover in which direction there were signs of a human settlement, etc. But at long last, when he did discover a straight path leading out of the wilderness, he thought, quite rightly, that it was a waste of time to teach about the ways of the forest to others who are also lost in the wilderness. It is most useful and urgent if he devoted his time and energy to point out the path to other suffering beings. This is exactly the function of a Buddha. Therefore he refrained from teaching what was irrelevant to emancipation. This clearly shows that the Buddha is far superior to other arahants regarding knowledge about matters not directly related to Nibbāna.

Among arahants too there are differences in attainment. In one place the Buddha states that in a group of 500 monks sixty are arahants with the six higher knowledges (*chaḷabhiññā*), sixty are arahants with the three clear knowledges (*tevijjā*), another sixty are arahants liberated from both parts (*ubhatobhāgavimutta*), while the rest are arahants liberated by wisdom (*paññāvimutta*).[7]

(1) The highest qualifications among arahants are the six higher knowledges (*chaḷabhiññā*) and the four analytical knowledges (*catupaṭisambhidā*).[8] The former comprise psychic powers, the divine ear, thought reading, retrocognition (the ability to recall one's former births), clairvoyance (the ability to see beings dying and being reborn according to their kamma), and the knowledge of the destruction of defilements. The four analytical knowledges comprise insight into the meaning of words (*attha*), truth (*dhamma*), use of language (*nirutti*), and originality of ideas (*paṭibhāna*). They seem to pivot round the ability to teach the Dhamma through the medium of verbal communication with appealing and meaningful ways of presentation.

(2) Arahants of lesser attainments have only three higher knowledges: retrocognition, clairvoyance, and the knowledge of the destruction of defilements.

(3) Still other arahants attain emancipation from both parts (*ubhatobhāgavimutti*). They have gained emancipation from the body (*rūpakāya*)[9] by the physical experience and complete mastery of eight "deliverances" (*vimokkhas*) or supernormal states of consciousness, and emancipation from the mind (*nāmakāya*)[10] through the destruction of defilements.

(4) Arahants who are released through wisdom have only the knowledge of the destruction of defilements. As a common denominator all arahants have *paññāvimutti*, also called *akuppā cetovimutti*, "imperturbable mental freedom."

While the highest qualities attainable by an arahant are certainly found in the Buddha,[11] the Suttas assign additional qualifications to the Buddha which are not shared by other arahants. The Mahāsīhanāda Sutta describes ten special powers of the Buddha called *tathāgatabala*.[12] They are tabulated below and will be taken up for discussion in comparison with the attainments of arahants. Endowed with these ten powers the Buddha claims a position of supreme eminence (*āsabhaṁ ṭhānaṁ paṭijānāti*). He is fearless in facing any audience or critic; the text metaphorically states that "he roars like a lion in assemblies" (*parisāsu sīhanādaṁ nadati*). He exercises supreme authority among human beings (*brahmacakkaṁ pavatteti*). The ten powers are as follows:

(1) He knows realistically a possibility as a possibility and an impossibility as an impossibility.

(2) He knows realistically the causally connected results of all actions whether they belong to the past, present, or future.

(3) He knows realistically the course of action leading to all states of existence.

(4) He knows realistically all worlds composed of various and diverse elements.

(5) He knows realistically the various spiritual propensities or dispositions of human beings.

(6) He knows realistically the maturity levels of the spiritual faculties of various human beings.

(7) He knows realistically the attainment of superconscious meditational levels such as *jhāna, vimokkha, samādhi,* and *samāpatti* together with the defilements and purities associated with them and the means of rising from these states.

(8) He has retrocognitive powers extending up to several aeons with ability to recall details regarding past existences.

(9) He has clairvoyant powers with the ability to see beings dying and being reborn in high or low states according to their own kamma.

(10) He has attained knowledge of the complete destruction of all defilements in this very life.

These will be taken up for discussion in comparison with the attainments of arahants, in reverse order as it seems to be clearer and more convenient to do so.

(10): The Buddha shares the last of the *tathāgatabalas* with all other arahants, and there seems to be no difference between the Buddha and the arahants in regard to emancipation.

(8) and (9): Arahants with the triple and sixfold higher knowledge share with the Buddha the retrocognitive and clairvoyant abilities. But there seems to be a difference in proficiency and extent of vision: the Buddha seems to have unlimited retrocognitive and clairvoyant abilities, as he says that he can see as far as he wishes to see (*yāvad eva ākaṅkhāmi*).[13]

(7): The Buddha shares his mastery over superconscious meditational levels with the *ubhatobhāgavimutta* arahant, who can attain the eight deliverances (*aṭṭha vimokkhā*) in progressive order, regressive order, and in both progressive and regressive orders; he can attain whatever he wishes, whenever he wishes, for any length of time he wishes, and can also rise from them at will.[14]

(5) and (6): These are special aspects of thought-reading (*cetopariyañāṇa*). Though arahants with *chaḷabhiññā* are said to have the ability of thought-reading, nowhere is it stated in the Pāli Canon that arahants can discern the spiritual propensities and maturity levels of the spiritual faculties of other individuals. This seems to be a special province of the Buddha alone. Much evidence could be gathered from the Pāli Canon in support of this special ability of the Buddha. Seeing the spiritual maturity of Angulimāla, Sunīta, and Ālavaka, the Buddha approached them on his own initiative.[15] He preached to them and they gained lasting spiritual distinction. There is not a single instance of an arahant approaching a prospective saint with prior knowledge of his spiritual potentialities. According to the Udāna the Buddha saw the

spiritual potential of a poor leper named Suppabuddha and preached a sermon which was particularly appealing to him.[16] At the end of the discourse he became a *sotāpanna,* a stream-enterer. According to the Cūḷarāhulovāda Sutta the Buddha saw that Rāhula was mature and ready for further instruction. He preached to Rāhula about the nature of sense faculties, sense data, and their interaction. At the end of this discourse, it is reported that Rāhula attained arahantship.[17] Countless other examples could be cited.

(2), (3), and (4): These seem to be specialities connected with clairvoyance (*dibbacakkhu*) . They show that the Buddha possesses a world view far superior to that of the arahants. With clairvoyance arahants realize only one aspect, the truth of kamma, which is so helpful for the understanding of man's *saṁsāric* condition. The Buddha's clairvoyance encompasses knowledge regarding the external world as well. Therefore he knows realistically the worlds with various and diverse elements. Perhaps this means that he has understood the universe comprising gross physical realms such as the human world, fine-material realms such as the Brahma-worlds, and non-material realms such as the *arūpa* world. He also knows the type of action which leads to rebirth in these various worlds, and he has understood the perennial laws pertaining to these worlds. His clairvoyant vision reaches so far back that he has recorded in the Mahāpadāna Sutta details regarding the lives of six previous Buddhas, much to the admiration of his followers.[18] In fact, as mentioned earlier in this essay, the Buddha's clairvoyant powers seem limitless.

(1): This special power of knowing a possibility as a possibility and an impossibility as an impossibility is never mentioned as a knowledge of the arahant. The Buddha may have left the "undetermined (*abyākata*) problems" unanswered because he was utterly convinced by this special form of insight that it is not only useless but impossible for unenlightened beings to know the solutions to those problems.

Besides the ten *tathāgatabalas* the Mahāsīhanāda Sutta enumerates four confidences (*cattāri vesārajjāni*) enjoyed by the Buddha alone.[19] He has the absolute confidence that no human or superhuman being can reasonably accuse him: (a) of not being fully enlightened; (b) of not being free of all mental defilements; (c) of wrongly declaring as dangers things that are not really dangerous; (d) of preaching a doctrine which does not lead to the goal it professes to lead to. Endowed with this absolute confidence the Buddha claims supreme eminence and authority among gods and men that no arahant could ever claim.

The Aṅguttara Nikāya enumerates ten powers of the arahant and they all seem to pivot round the practice and realization of the Dhamma:[20]

(1) An arahant sees all component things as impermanent.
(2) He sees all sense pleasures as a pit of burning embers.
(3) His mind is inclined towards seclusion and renunciation.
(4) He has developed the four stations of mindfulness.
(5) He has developed the fourfold right exertion.
(6) He has developed the four bases of psychic powers.
(7) He has developed the five spiritual faculties.
(8) He has developed the five spiritual powers.
(9) He has developed the seven factors of enlightenment.
(10) He has developed the Noble Eightfold Path.

Endowed with these powers a monk can claim to have destroyed all mental defilements. When compared with the powers and confidences of the Buddha, these centre round the theme of one's own individual emancipation. The Buddha, on the other hand, wields far greater powers which can even be called universal, with insight into the spiritual potential of other individuals and a world view far superior to that of arahants.

It is appropriate to compare the epithets which normally describe an arahant with those applied to the Buddha. Suttas describe an arahant as *khīṇāsavo*, "one whose mental defilements are destroyed"; *vusitavā*, "one who has successfully lived the higher life"; *katakaraṇīyo*, "one whose duty is done"; *ohitabhāro*, "one who has laid the burden aside"; *anuppattasadattho*, "one who has attained the noble goal"; *parikkhīṇabhavasaṁyojano*, "one who has destroyed all bonds leading to further existences"; and *sammadaññāvimutto*, "one who has attained emancipation with right knowledge."[21] All these epithets describe aspects of the personal emancipation of the arahant. Though all these epithets can rightly be applied to the Buddha, they are hardly used with reference to him as it is not just his personal emancipation that makes him unique.

The Buddha's fame spread in terms of nine other epithets. He is called *arahaṁ*, as he is the worthy one who does no evil even in secret; *sammā-sambuddho*, because he is fully enlightened and self-enlightened; *vijjācaraṇasampanno*, because he is endowed with knowledge and (virtuous) conduct; *sugato*, because he successfully reached the goal as a pioneer; *lokavidū*, because he has understood the universe with its world systems; *purisadammasārathī*, because he is the champion tamer of human beings; *satthā devamanussānaṁ*, because he is the teacher of gods and men; *buddho*, because he has awakened to reality; *bhagavā*, because he is the fortunate one, the Blessed One, the lord.[22] Though a few of these epithets could be attributed to the arahant as well, this group of nine epithets collectively expresses the praiseworthy qualities of the Buddha alone. In their totality they can never be applied to an arahant.

To emphasize his superiority, the Buddha himself declares that even those monks who are liberated in mind and who have achieved "unsurpassed vision, unsurpassed practice, and unsurpassed liberation" still honour, respect, esteem, and worship the Buddha. The reason is: "The Blessed One is enlightened, and teaches the Dhamma for enlightenment; he is tamed, and teaches the Dhamma for taming; he is at peace, and teaches the Dhamma for peace; he has attained Nibbāna, and teaches the Dhamma for attaining Nibbāna."[23]

The Buddha has sometimes referred to himself as *sabbābhibhū*,[24] because he has conquered everything, all passions. Though the Buddha acknowledges himself to be *sabbavidū*,[25] "all-knowing", he has rejected the epithet *sabbaññū* which also has the same meaning.[26] At the time of the Buddha *sabbaññū* had a special connotation as Nigaṇṭha Nātaputta, the founder of Jainism, also claimed to be *sabbaññū*.[27] Nātaputta claimed to have ever-present continuous knowledge of everything all the time whether he was awake or asleep. The Buddha disclaims such ever-present continuous knowledge of everything. In fact he maintains that no one can ever have knowledge of everything at one and the same time.[28] It is an impossibility.

It is possible to interpret the "all-knowing" (*sabbavidū*) aspect of the Buddha's knowledge in terms of the definition of *sabba*, "all, everything" as given in the Sabba Sutta.[29] According to this definition "everything" means the five sense faculties and their corresponding objects, plus the mind and the corresponding mental phenomena. In this sutta the Buddha challenges anybody to give a more comprehensive definition of "everything." The Buddha's ability to know something was such that he had to direct his attention to the desired object in order to know it as it really is. The Buddha clearly says that he can recollect as far back as he wishes through his retrocognitive knowledge, and his clairvoyant abilities are similarly wish-bound. He does not have a mirror-like knowledge or vision where everything is automatically reflected. Here we are reminded of the incident when the Buddha decided to preach the Dhamma.[30] He thought of Āḷāra Kālāma first to preach the Dhamma to, but he did not know that Āḷāra had died a week ago. Then he thought of Uddaka Rāmaputta only to realize that he too had passed away the previous night. These episodes clearly show that the Buddha had to direct his attention if he wished to know something.

These episodes bring us to the interesting question whether it is possible for others to read the mind of the Buddha. When the Buddha was disinclined to preach the doctrine, Sahampati the great Brahmā immediately knew this and he came and requested the Buddha to preach.[31] According to the Brahmasaṁyutta, when the Buddha decided to honour the Dhamma as his teacher, because he saw none capable of being his teacher in the whole world of gods and men, Brahmā Sahampati appeared once again and informed him that this was the custom of previous Buddhas too, and Buddhas in the future also will do the same.[32] When the Buddha thought of choosing Āḷāra Kālāma and Uddaka Rāmaputta to be his first disciples, gods informed him of their death.[33] The Khandhasaṁyutta records another incident when Mahābrahmā read the thoughts of the Buddha and appeared before him to plead on behalf of some errant monks.[34] According to the Mahāparinibbāna Sutta, when the Buddha was going through the jhānic process in ascending and descending orders just before attaining *parinibbāna*, Anuruddha knew the jhānic process he was going through.[35] All these episodes point to the fact that at least certain aspects of the Buddha's mind were accessible to other arahants with thought-reading ability and certain superhuman beings.

Another episode recorded in the Mahāparinibbāna Sutta shows that all aspects of the Buddha's mind are not known even to the most eminent arahants.[36] Sāriputta once told the Buddha that he was convinced that there has never been, there will never be, and there is not at present any other recluse or brahmin who is more distinguished in enlightenment than the Buddha. The Buddha then asked Sāriputta whether he had read the minds of all past, present, and future Buddhas and known their virtue to be such and such (*evaṁsīlā*), their concentration to be such and such (*evaṁdhammā*), their wisdom to be such and such (*evaṁpaññā*), their mode of living to be such and such (*evaṁvihārī*), and their emancipation to be such and such (*evaṁvimuttā*). Sāriputta replied that he has no such knowledge and that he was only making a reasonable inference. All this evidence clearly points to the fact that there is no human or superhuman being, not even an arahant, who can fully read the mind of the Buddha, but of course the Buddha has the ability to read the minds of all others including arahants.

The Pāli Canon mentions five types of vision that the Buddha has. The first is *maṁsacakkhu*, the normal human vision consisting of the physical faculty of sight. According to the Lakkhaṇa Sutta the Buddha possesses a perfect pair of deep blue eyes with long eye lashes, because as a human being fulfilling the perfections requisite for Buddhahood he looked at others with pleasant kind eyes, honest and uncritical eyes.[37] The second type of vision is *dibbacakkhu*, the divine vision or clairvoyance, the most important function of which is the ability to see the passing away and rebirth of beings according to their respective kamma. The third is *paññācakkhu*, the vision of insight, which enabled the Buddha to see things as they really are, the impermanent, unsatisfactory, and non-substantial nature of everything.[38] The fourth is *buddhacakkhu*, the Buddha vision;[39] when the Buddha surveyed the world with this vision he saw people with a lesser and a greater degree of defilements, people with refined and dull spiritual faculties. The fifth is *samantacakkhu*, which we venture to translate as pan-vision.[40] It is possible to infer that this vision refers to the ability to see a problem or an issue in its entirety, as *samanta* means entire or all-round. Moreover, Mahābrahmā addresses the Buddha as *samantacakkhu* when he entreats him in allegorical terms to ascend to the top of the "Dhamma mansion" and behold the suffering mass of humanity.[41] The last two visions are never attributed to arahants and remain the sole province of the Buddha.

The Pāli Canon contains interesting material to draw a distinction between the enlightenment experience of the Buddha and that of the arahant. The Chabbisodhana Sutta enumerates several criteria of arahantship, which give a clear idea of what the Buddha expected of his disciples who have reached the ultimate goal of realization.[42] These criteria comprise the unshakeable freedom of the mind from the influence of the senses, from hankering after the constituents of personality, from craving for elements constituting the world, from the yearning for the internal and external sense spheres, and from the bias of the notion of "I" and "mine."[43] One of the most comprehensive accounts of the enlightenment experience of an arahant is given in the Mahā Assapura Sutta.[44] According to this the adept who has attained to the fourth jhāna gains first retrocognition and then clairvoyance. Then he directs his mind to the knowledge of the destruction of defilements. In this process he gains first-hand knowledge of suffering, its cause, its elimination, and the path leading to its elimination. He understands what mental defilements are, their origin, cessation, and the path leading to their cessation. When knowing thus, the mind (*citta*) is freed from the defilements of sense pleasures, desire for continued existence, and ignorance. In him who is released thus there arises the knowledge of freedom: birth is destroyed, the higher life has been successfully lived, one's duty has been done, there is no more of this continued existence. Just as a man standing beside a pool of clear unsullied water would see the shells, pebbles, and fish in the water, the adept would see, clearly and directly, suffering, its cause, its cessation, and the path leading to its cessation.

This could very well be a description of the Buddha's enlightenment experience too. But scattered in the Pāli Canon there are various biographical descriptions of his enlightenment which suggest that the above was only one of its aspects. It appears that the Buddha's enlightenment was a full, multifaceted, rich experience that could be explained from various angles. In the Mahāsaccaka Sutta the Buddha relates that he realized retrocognition during the first watch of the night, clairvoyance during the second watch, and the knowledge of the destruction of defilements during the third watch.[45] Therefore it is clear that enlightenment is not a sudden flash, but a gradual unfolding of human potentialities when conditions for it are ripe. It can be compared to the gradual unfolding of petals in the blossoming of a flower.

In the Khandhasaṁyutta the Buddha says: "So long as I did not understand the satisfaction (*assāda*), the evil consequences (*ādīnava*), and the escape (*nissaraṇa*) from the five aggregates of grasping, so long I did not claim supreme enlightenment."[46] The Mahāpadāna Sutta states that the mind (of Vipassi Buddha) attained emancipation from defilements when contemplating the rise and fall of the five aggregates of grasping.[47] Thus knowledge and vision into the five aggregates is another aspect of the enlightenment experience.

According to the Vedanāsaṁyutta, the Buddha did not claim enlightenment until he gained full vision into all aspects of feelings: what is feeling, what is its origin, its cessation, the path leading to its cessation, its satisfaction, its evil consequences, and escape therefrom.[48] As all beings are bound to *saṁsāra* because of their attachment to pleasures, and pleasures are but pleasurable sensations, it is only too logical that one has to have a thorough knowledge of all sensations (including pleasurable sensations) if one wants to make an end of *saṁsāra*. Therefore the Buddha's enlightenment experience comprised a thoroughgoing realization of all aspects of feeling too.

The Saḷāyatanasaṁyutta records another aspect.[49] According to this the Buddha did not claim enlightenment in the world of gods and men so long as he did not realistically understand the six sense faculties and their respective objects according to the satisfaction they yield, the evil consequences they entail, and the escape therefrom. As we are attached to pleasures through the instrumentality of our sense organs, in order to gain release we have to understand the nature of the sense faculties, sense objects, and their interrelationship. In the Nidānasaṁyutta the Buddha says that vision and knowledge arose in him regarding matters not heard of before (*ananussutesu dhammesu*) as he contemplated the *paṭiccasamuppāda*, paying attention to the causal process giving rise to suffering and the causal process bringing about the cessation of suffering.[50] The Aṅguttara Nikāya explains the gradual deepening of *dibbacakkhu*, clairvoyance, as an aspect of the enlightenment experience.[51] There are eight stages in this process of gradual development extending from pre-enlightenment days up to the enlightenment. The Buddha says that so long as he did not understand these eight stages, he did not claim enlightenment in the world of gods and men.

The most important and the most famous account of the enlightenment experience of the Buddha is recorded in the Vinaya Mahāvagga and this comprises the full comprehension of the Four Noble Truths.[52] As this statement is of great significance it is recorded below in detail. The Buddha says that:

(1) (i) Wisdom and knowledge arose in him regarding truths never heard of before and he was able to isolate the problem of the noble truth of suffering; (ii) he understood that the truth of suffering must be fully comprehended, and (iii) that the truth of suffering has been fully comprehended.

(2) (i) Wisdom and knowledge arose in him regarding the cause of suffering; (ii) he understood that this cause of suffering must be eliminated, and (iii) that this cause of suffering has been eliminated.

(3) (i) Wisdom and knowledge arose in him that the cessation of suffering is a possibility; (ii) he understood that the cessation of suffering must be realized, and (iii) that the cessation of suffering has been realized.

(4) (i) Wisdom and knowledge arose in him regarding the path leading to the cessation of suffering; (ii) he understood that this path must be developed, and (iii) that this path has been developed.

The Buddha says that he did not claim to have attained supreme enlightenment until he realized the Four Noble Truths each according to the threefold ramifications (*tiparivaṭṭaṁ*); thus the four truths run into twelve details (*dvādasākāraṁ*). This was such a novel realization that he uses the phrase "truths never heard of before" (*pubbe ananussutesu dhammesu*) with each of the above twelve statements. The wisdom that arose was so profound that he uses five terms to describe different aspects of this deep spiritual awakening: "vision arose" (*cakkhuṁ udapādi*), "wisdom arose" (*ñāṇaṁ udapādi*), "insight arose" (*paññā udapādi*), "knowledge arose" (*vijjā udapādi*), and "illumination arose" (*āloko udapādi*).

We are now in a position to compare the enlightenment experience of the arahant with that of the Buddha. The Mahā

Assapura account cited earlier in this essay, which can be regarded as one of the best descriptions of an arahant's enlightenment experience, seems to fade into insignificance when compared with the rich, multifaceted enlightenment experience of the Buddha. Nowhere has the Pāli Canon attributed insight into the sense faculties, sense objects, sensations, etc., *as an enlightenment experience* of an arahant. As stated in the Chabbisodhana Sutta it is very probable that they realistically understand the nature of sense faculties, sense objects, elements, etc., that these phenomena are impermanent, unsatisfactory, and non-substantial,[53] but they may not gain insight into the inner workings of these phenomena. The arahant's enlightenment experience is introduced by the phrase *yathābhūtaṁ pajānāti*, "realistically understands," whereas the Buddha's enlightenment experience is expressed as "vision arose, wisdom arose, insight arose, knowledge arose, illumination arose." The Pāli Canon never uses this phraseology to refer to the realization of an arahant. The realization of the Four Noble Truths by an arahant is also expressed in terms of realistic understanding.[54] But the Buddha's vision into the Four Truths is described in twelve details consisting of the threefold ramifications with respect to each of the Four Truths. The simile used in the Mahā Assapura Sutta to describe the enlightenment experience of the arahant is that of a pond of crystal-clear water where a man standing on its bank sees the pebbles, shells, etc., in its bed and shoals of fish swimming in the water.[55] But the Buddha's enlightenment experience is like the panoramic view one gets from the summit of a mountain, and this is exactly the imagery Mahābrahmā uses to describe the Buddha's enlightenment experience.[56]

We are not in a position to conjecture whether the various facets of the enlightenment experience of the Buddha had a chronological and a hierarchical order, and if so what that order was. It could also have been an experience like circular vision, as when one is at the top of a mountain where the scenery on the east is different from the scenery in the west, and the scenery in the north different from that of the south. However different the sceneries may be from the different directions, all the scenes constitute one integrated experience of a person standing on a vantage point. The scanty evidence gleaned from the Pāli Canon seems to favour a combination of both these patterns for the Buddha's enlightenment experience. The experience has started with a chronological hierarchy, as according to the Mahāsaccaka Sutta the higher knowledges of retrocognition, clairvoyance, and the destruction of defilements were realized during the first, second, and third watches of the night respectively.[57] The other facets of the enlightenment experience may be parts of the spiritual panorama seen in different directions from the vantage point of reality. Whatever the pattern may be, an arahant's enlightenment is a much less significant, much less dramatic experience than that of the Buddha, which is so profound, multifaceted, rich, and unique.

In conclusion it can be stated that the Buddha would have realized a far more profound world view than he chose to preach to humanity. As that knowledge was far too complicated for ordinary comprehension, and as it was irrelevant for the solution of the human problem of suffering, keeping that profound knowledge as the framework within which to work, the Buddha would have preached to humanity how best we could order our life in order to achieve harmony and peace in such a world. This harmony at the highest level is Nibbāna. Those who followed him lacked the profound world view, but learnt the practice for the attainment of lasting peace and emancipation.

Notes

1. M III 7–15.
2. M I 225–27.
3. J I 19 ff.
4. S V 438.
5. *Desito Ānanda mayā dhammo anantaraṁ abāhiraṁ karitvā, natthi tathāgatassa dhammesu ācariyamuṭṭhi*: D II 100.
6. M I 140; S I 135, III 119, V 384.
7. S I 191.
8. A II 160.
9. See Lily de Silva, "Cetovimutti, Paññāvimutti, and Ubhatobhāgavimutti," *Pali Buddhist Review*, Vol. 3, No. 3. 1978, pp.142–43.
10. Ibid.
11. M I 22–23, 117, 248–49.
12. M I 68–83.
13. M I 482.
14. D II 71.
15. M II 98–99; Thag 620–31; Sn p.31.
16. Ud pp. 48–51.
17. M III 277–80.
18. D II 2 ff.; see M III 118.
19. M I 71.
20. A V 174–76.
21. M I 141.
22. D I 49, 87, 111, etc.
23. M I 235.
24. Vin I 8; M I 171.
25. Ibid.

26. M I 482.
27. M II 31.
28. *Natthi so samaṇo vā brāhmaṇo vā yo sakid eva sabbaṁ nāssati sabbaṁ dakkhiti n'etaṁ ṭhānaṁ vijjatīti*: M II 127.
29. S IV 15.
30. M I 170.
31. M I 168.
32. S I 139.
33. M I 170.
34. S III 91.
35. D II 156.
36. D II 82; S V 159.
37. D II 167.
38. S IV 292, V 467; A I 35.
39. Vin I 6 = S I 138.
40. M I 168.
41. Ibid.
42. M III 29–37.
43. Karel Werner, "Bodhi and Arahattaphala: From Early Buddhism to Early Mahāyāna." *The Journal of the International Association of Buddhist Studies*, Vol. 4, No. 1, 1981, p.76.
44. M I 278–79.
45. M I 248.
46. S III 27.
47. D II 35.
48. S IV 233.
49. S IV 7–10.
50. S II 10.

51. A IV 302–5.

52. Vin I 10 = S V 422, 436.

53. M III 29–37.

54. *Yathābhūtaṁ pajānāti* : M I 62, 279.

55. M I 279.

56. *Sele yathā pabbatamuddhaniṭṭhito*: M I 168.

57. M I 248–49.

KEY TO ABBREVIATIONS

A	Aṅguttara Nikāya
D	Dīgha Nikāya
Dh	Dhammapada
DhA	Dhammapada Aṭṭhakathā
J	Jātakas
M	Majjhima Nikāya
MA	Majjhima Nikāya Aṭṭhakathā
Miln	Milindapañha
S	Saṁyutta Nikāya
SA	Saṁyutta Nikāya Aṭṭhakathā
Sn	Suttanipāta
Thag	Theragāthā
ThagA	Theragāthā Aṭṭhakathā
Thig	Therīgāthā
Ud	Udāna
Vin	Vinaya
VinA	Vinaya Aṭṭhakathā
Vsm	Visuddhimagga

Also from BPS

The Questions of King Milinda

An Abridgement of the Milindapañha

Edited by N.K.G. Mendis

One of the most sublime works of Buddhist literature, *The Questions of King Milinda* is an imaginative record of a series of discussions between the Bactrian Greek King Milinda, who reigned in the Punjab, and the Buddhist sage Bhante Nāgasena. Their spirited dialogue—dramatic and witty, eloquent and inspired—explores the diverse problems of Buddhist thought and practice from the perspective of a probing Greek intellectual who is both perplexed and fascinated by the strangely rational religion he discovered on the Indian subcontinent. The present abridged edition has been adapted from existing scholarly translations, and includes in an easily readable style the most essential passages of the original classic.

Softback: 208 pages
U.S. $10; SL Rs. 280

140 mm x 214 mm
Order No. BP 217S

THE BUDDHIST PUBLICATION SOCIETY

The BPS is an approved charity dedicated to making known the Teaching of the Buddha, which has a vital message for people of all creeds. Founded in 1958, the BPS has published a wide variety of books and booklets covering a great range of topics. Its publications include accurate annotated translations of the Buddha's discourses, standard reference works, as well as original contemporary expositions of Buddhist thought and practice. These works present Buddhism as it truly is—a dynamic force which has influenced receptive minds for the past 2500 years and is still as relevant today as it was when it first arose. A full list of our publications will be sent upon request with an enclosure of U.S. $1.50 or its equivalent to cover air mail postage. Write to:

The Hony. Secretary
BUDDHIST PUBLICATION SOCIETY
P.O. Box 61
54, Sangharaja Mawatha
Kandy • Sri Lanka